KELLY CRAWFORD

Think Outside the Classroom

A Practical Approach to
Relaxed Homeschooling

Table of Contents

Think Outside the Classroom:

Introduction

"If a student can be led to the tools he needs to answer his own questions, he will be always learning; and this should be the goal of every educator."

⌘ ⌘ ⌘

Every starry-eyed homeschooling Mom begins with great expectations. I know I did. I walked out of a classroom teaching high school English, right into our classroom at home. There my daughter sat primly in her student desk; we recited the pledge of allegiance, asked questions only with raised hand, and I stood with a long, pointy stick aimed at the alphabet chart behind me. This was going to be **wonderful**!

Then my bubble burst. She was bored. I was frustrated. Neither of us was having much fun. It became drudgery. This was NOT what I had pictured! "Oh dear, this is what I must resign to... a lifetime of force-feeding information to my non-interested children. I knew I couldn't do it!"

What I had yet to learn was that copying "it" at home was only one of many options in homeschooling. The freedom of home taught me that education looked different for every family and even every child. We were "doing school" in those first weeks, but I wasn't sure how much she was actually learning.

I am so happy to report that, today, twelve years later, our homeschool looks a lot different. We love homeschooling, we are relaxed, and my kids (and myself) are learning by leaps and bounds. Instead of depending on someone to feed them information, they are learning how to learn. And I write this book to give you hope for your homeschool experience!

We are what some would call "relaxed" homeschoolers. I have come to love and see the benefits of a relaxed approach to learning, and I

> *"If you don't know where you are going, any road will get you there."*
>
> Lewis Carrol

can't wait to share our experience with you. If your family has a "system", and it works for you, your children are truly being educated, and you're not under a lot of stress, I would suggest you keep it.

But if you find homeschooling to be more of a burden than a joy, perhaps it's time to try a different approach. A friend once said to me, *"Being a mother is hard work. But if God gave us these children to nurture and teach, surely He didn't mean for it to be impossible!"*

Please don't misunderstand me; we are a normal family with the same challenges every family faces. We deal with bad attitudes (children and mom's!), disobedience and strife, just like you do. And we have bad days. But aside from the normal part of working together through those things as a family, we have grown to understand that learning has many faces. Homeschooling doesn't have to be misery and drudgery.

Many moms have said to me, *"I love the concept of relaxed schooling, but I have no idea how to do it — what it looks like."* Those comments are what prompted me to write this book. I'm going to show you what it looks like for us, and hopefully inspire you to explore what it can look like for your family.

Think Outside the Classroom:

Chapter 1:
Education — Building the Framework

Thinking Outside the Box

So much of the homeschooling experience involves "unlearning." Because most of us went to public or private school, we have this idea — and rightly so since it's all we ever knew — that education can only be accomplished one way. We basically all think that students sitting in rows of desks with a teacher transferring her knowledge to them is the best, and possibly the only way to learn. Or maybe we've never given it much thought. Or maybe we know it's not the best way, but we are afraid to alter the course because then we wouldn't be doing what everyone else is doing.

John Taylor Gatto, a retired 30-year veteran teacher-of-the-year in the New York City school system, publicly speaks out against the "injury" he says institutionalized schooling inflicts on children. His insight into the way we've schooled for so many years has radically changed the way I view our homeschooling:

> *"Children learn what they live. Put kids in a class and they will live out their lives in an invisible cage, isolated from their chance at community; interrupt kids with bells and horns all the time and they will learn that nothing is important or worth finishing... The habits taught in large-scale organizations are deadly."* John Taylor Gatto

Stepping out of the mainstream, daring to do something different requires a certain amount of faith; faith in the results, in those who have gone before us, and in the intuition God has given us to parent. But the results of taking that leap of faith is so rewarding. After awhile, the fears and doubts subside, and you can see that the fears had no merit after all.

What is Education?

Instead of duplicating the only method we knew regarding how to "do school", we backed up and began to ask ourselves the simple question: *"What is education?"* In order to begin building, we must know what we're building in the first place. A storage shed and a cathedral are going to have very different-looking blueprints. Most parents fail to realize that the structure the state is trying to design is in the shape of a **test**. Tests are the gauge schools use to determine their success. And while a test can be an important tool for assessing progress, it should not be the end-all for determining the method.

Additionally, we need to realize tests can only measure limited outcomes, mostly related to memorization. Education encompasses far more than what a child can memorize, but tests are not able to measure the vast and varied thing known as "education."

So, if we teach solely for the purpose of achieving a desired test score, we have missed the entire purpose of education. So much of the current methods of compulsory schooling involve heaping unrelated information upon students in order that they can score higher on a test. But how many public high school graduates do you know can articulate his thoughts about philosophy, theology or other significant matters? Are they teaching our children to think? To discern truth and wisdom? To do things, to work hard, to really be prepared for the real world? To live life doing things that matter?

The Standardized Myth

This emphasis on testing has reinforced a crippling myth that almost all of us seem to embrace: the myth that all children need to learn the same things. Certainly there are basics, formally known as "the 3 R's." But beyond these basics, which children will learn quite naturally, education is many things to many people. Not everyone needs to have a solid grasp of interpreting Shakespeare. Some will naturally gravitate to that, and should be given all the opportunity they wish for such study. Some will be brilliant mechanical thinkers and should be given equal time to pursue that knowledge. Some are artists, some musicians, some will do a little of everything. But it's my firm belief that we must stop treating differences outside of the "standard curriculum" as sub-par or extra-curricular. We need to give our children freedom to pursue *their* education.

For us, education has much more to do with nurturing the mind than it does with any memorization of facts.

Gatto, in his excellent book *A Different Kind of Teacher*, writes:

> *"A study of any list of great men and women will quickly disclose the host of personal methods they used to arrive at personal enlightenment—an education. No one I know ever gave much credit to the daily doses of abstraction prescribed by strangers and imposed on his life by compulsion (modern schooling). But plenty of autobiographies credit a mother, a father, a grandmother, a grandfather, an uncle, an aunt, or*

a chance accident happened upon while adventuring
Maybe there's a lesson there."

As parents who have been given the responsibility of educating and discipling our children (Deuteronomy 6[1]), we can't get this wrong. We have to clearly outline our educational goals and then pursue the best path for achieving them. As Christians, this should mean, above all, that we are far more concerned with eternal things. So often, the reality that we do live in a society that operates within certain bounds overtakes our spiritual duty to raise up men and women who love and serve the Lord. **No preparation, no level of education or training can compensate for our failure to do that.**

John Mark Reynolds, Philosopher of Education and homeschooling dad writes:

> *"First, education must begin and end with virtue... Too often home educators try to set up a government school at home. How foolish I was with all my records, charts, tests, and clip boards at the start!"*

He also simplified education well:

> *"Students should read well, write well, be numerate, and cultured."*

---

1 "Now this is the commandment, and these are the statutes and judgments which the Lord your God has commanded to teach you... And these words which I command you today shall be in your heart. You shall teach them diligently to your children, and shall talk of them when you sit in your house, when you walk by the way, when you lie down, and whenyou rise up."

Think Outside the Classroom:

Our Educational Objectives

We have basically outlined the following objectives for our children. Yours may be different:

1. To teach them the fear of the Lord as the foundation of knowledge
2. To teach them to be self-learners
3. To teach them how to think
4. To teach them how to effectively communicate
5. To encourage them to love to read
6. To teach them to be productive
7. To teach them to understand math
8. To teach them to love the arts

A Word About Relationships

So often I've seen parents trying to implement their idea of what homeschooling should be, even to the detriment of the relationships with their children. I believe if my children learned **nothing** except how to love the Lord, and we had their hearts, I would consider it a successful homeschool experience.

No academic goal is worth losing the priceless relationships with our children. I've advised frustrated mothers to "take off" for the remainder of the year and focus on building relationships. Once those are established, homeschooling gets so much easier! And to borrow from the Scriptural concept, "What does it profit a man to gain the world and lose his own soul?" I ask, "What does it profit a parent to raise studious children and lose their hearts?"

> ## Idea Corner
> To keep the attention of little ones while reading, collect old magazines (nature-type are good) and let them cut and glue (with a glue stick!) pictures onto construction paper. After reading, you can talk about each picture with them for an extra learning opportunity.

Chapter 2:
A Lifestyle of Learning

I will explain how our family seeks to accomplish our educational objectives in detail in the next chapter, but first I want to explain some simple, but often overlooked precepts about the process of learning. It is these foundational principles that will change the way we approach education.

A term I think accurately defines the relaxed homeschool method is "lifestyle of learning." We believe that learning is a continual process, with no starting or stopping point. We believe that everything in a day has teaching merit, and should be viewed as a learning opportunity. Consider these learning foundations:

Curiosity: The Key to Real-life Education

At the core of this idea of relaxed homeschooling is a simple, yet largely overlooked fact: God instilled in each person a natural curiosity meant to guide and gravitate him toward learning things he needs for life. Simply put, a child is born with everything he needs to obtain a meaningful and thorough education. All he needs is the exposure to information and to be taught how to use that information.

Far too often we squelch the very nature of a child's curiosity with our notions of schooling. Is it any wonder why there is an epidemic of children being drugged to make it through a school day? More often than not, these children aren't plagued with illness; they are simply children, made to explore, move about, find answers to their questions using their five senses, being separated from the world, confined to a sterile environment, and force-fed information that doesn't interest them. I don't think there is an epidemic of ADHD in American schools; I think there is an epidemic of boredom. Let's not repeat the tragedy.

Consider how a child learns language. I don't know a parent who began a rigorous language course with their infant. But consider how crucial it is for him to learn to communicate. And yet, I've never seen a parent wringing hands over his baby's crib, worried that he is not going to get the proper tutoring for this important life skill.

Why? Because God designed that infant to be strangely curious, with a strong desire to get what he wants. He learns by observation about the human language. It is spoken to him, long before he understands each symbol and meaning of the words. If you think about it, it's almost miraculous that, at about the age of 1, he begins to imitate sounds of words. And by the time he is two, he has a rather impressive vocabulary.

Amazing! No "teacher", no curriculum, and yet he learns one of the most complicated systems on the planet. This demonstration of the mind is no different than how a person learns everything else. The baby was repeatedly exposed to information, he had a need/desire to learn it, and with no forcing at all, accomplished the task. I submit one can receive an entire education based on that same concept. Better yet, I believe it is a superior form of learning.

Parents have been misled into thinking that young children must undergo some regiment to prepare for school. The term "learning readiness" is a buzz word now. But just as God's ways have always been putting to shame the world's ways, this one is no exception. People are born "ready to learn."

All too often, we take that same little curious brain, that mind that loves to learn, that can't wait to explore the world around him, and we squish it into a box and a time-frame. Tragically, we squelch his God-given love of learning. And in just a few years, we have literally taught the child that he can only learn if someone else imparts information to him. Furthermore, we teach him there's an appropriate time to learn, with starting and stopping points. Most children loathe "learning" by the time they reach high school age.

What if we were able to preserve that in-born curiosity, that ability to soak up information simply by hearing, seeing and touching it? What would that do to the way we view education?

Importance of Quiet Time & Solitude

Another one of those overly simple things that gets overlooked is the importance of a child just having quiet time to explore, think and create. So he's outside playing in the mud with a stick? Leave him for a time. It's a good thing for a child to be alone with his thoughts, to experiment with his world, to observe "cause and effect" and the laws of nature around him. Our culture is a noisy one where we feel the need to be constantly entertained, busy or occupied. This busyness can rob our children of an important part of education. A child's soul cannot grow without some silence and solitude.

> *"Good things happen to the human spirit when it is left alone."*
> *John Taylor Gatto*

I fear one of the greatest losses to technology has been the death of solitude. Being still, being quiet and alone with one's thoughts is a crucial, missing element for today's child, and the constant over-stimulation is damaging to the brain, actually causing a short attention span and lowered ability to retain information.

Conversation

One of the most important tools in a parent's hands for teaching his children is conversation. Dialog is a missing ingredient from a typical classroom. It's overlooked because it seems too simple; but keep my language analogy in mind.

Dialog, or conversation, is vitally important to education and to human existence itself. Tragically, the constant access to television, video games, computers and devices keeps us so distracted we are losing the art of conversation. Worse yet, as our ability to verbally communicate diminishes, so does our power to defend our faith to the world around us.

As I talk to even my youngest children throughout the day, I try to engage them verbally and intellectually. When we go for a walk, whether I'm with my two-year old or my fourteen year old, I point out as many details about things we see as I can. For example, my two-year old naturally sees the bright red flower, so she stops to ooh and ahh over it.

"Fower, mommy," she says.

"Yes, that's a red clover... isn't it pretty? I think the colors are brilliant, don't you? Bees like red clover."

I may go on and on, using different words besides "brilliant", so she hears a variety of words with the same meaing. Silly? Think back to how we talk to a child who hasn't yet learned to speak. We repeat things. And the more they hear them, the more they learn. Use some words that are above your child's understanding... remember, all words used to be above his understanding! This is a real, living education.

Ask Questions

An important part of the conversation is also questioning. Asking questions and finding answers is the most basic definition of education. Instead of forcing our children to memorize someone else's thoughts about a subject, we need to push them to develop some of their own, analyzing, observing and concluding based on their personal experiences about the world around them.

"Sit down before fact as a little child, be prepared to give up every preconceived notion, follow humbly wherever or whatever abysses nature leads, or you will learn nothing."

Thomas H. Huxley

After embracing the importance of conversation for some time, I recently heard Geoffrey Botkin, a father of five brilliant children who are having a huge impact on our culture through writing books and creating media products, say, *"Most of our homeschooling was simply conversation."*

Pay Attention

A lifestyle of learning is mostly a matter of paying attention to opportunities. What questions are they asking? What questions can you ask them? Many times my children will ask a question to which I don't know the answer. It can be tempting (and sometimes is necessary) to put them off with an "I don't know." But it's much better to say, "I don't know... but come with me and we'll find the answer!"

Between books that we continually collect, the library, the dictionary and the Internet, we can usually find the answer we're looking for. **Get into the habit of asking questions and finding answers. This is really the foundation for all learning!**

And if you are in the middle of something that can't be put off, keep a running list of interests your child has shown, and look them up when you get a chance. It's not as good as seizing the moment, but better than forgetting altogether.

Idea Corner

Pick a "word of the day" and see how many times you can use it in the day, and encourage your children to do the same. Make up a song about the word. While reading Winnie the Pooh, I ran across the word "revolving." I stopped and said, "Do you know what revolving means? It means to go in circles, or spin around." And then I asked one of my children to stand in the middle of the floor and spin in circles. While she did that, I sang a chorus to the tune of "A Tisket, a Tasket" that went: "Revolving, revolving...Alexa is revolving...'round and 'round, she spins around, Alexa is revolving."

Chapter 3:
How We Implement
Our Objectives

The details of how we implement this lifestyle of learning, ultimately achieving our educational objectives, are below. These are merely suggestions and starting points. Every family is different, with different opportunities and goals. Let them be a springboard for your ideas.

Teaching the Fear of the Lord

Above all else, we want them to love the Lord with all their hearts. If you get anything from this book, I would hope that you get this: *"The fear of the Lord is the beginning of knowledge."*

I submit that a child, no matter how much he is taught, cannot have a true education apart from this fundamental fear of and love for the Lord. Period. This is one of the reasons that we would go to jail before we let government education be forced upon our children. We live in a culture of "falsely educated" people. People with knowledge but no truth--possibly the most dangerous element of a society.

I cannot underestimate the importance of teaching God's Word to our children. There are many wonderful tools and resources to help parents impart Biblical truths, but there is **nothing** that tops the Bible itself. (It is a given, of course, that Mom and Dad living out Christian faith in front of their children is paramount to imparting a biblical worldview.)

The inspired Word of God is under serious attack, even within the church. We must be vigilant to defend it, and to teach our children to do the same. Without a solid understanding of the principles and doctrines taught in Scripture, they will be susceptible to the subtle deceptions that are infiltrating the church. And regardless of who else is assisting you in this task, it is your primary responsibility and must be deliberately executed.

We make a tragic mistake assuming that the Bible is too hard for our little ones to understand, and thus postpone the daily reading of it to them. It's fine to read the children's version of Jonah and the Whale, but be sure to read the original story from the Bible too.

We read a book once called *Ten Peas in a Pod*. The father of the family in the book was an incredible man. The reading of God's Word aloud, to his family every day, was the single highest priority on his agenda. It got done if nothing else did. And he mentioned that he usually even woke up the baby to sit in on the reading!

I couldn't believe that. But then he explained, just like my earlier analogy of how a child learns language, that if we postponed speaking to a child until he was old enough to understand the words, linguistically, he would be greatly impaired. The same is true of his spiritual understanding. A person who has not heard the regular reading of God's Word until he is old enough to understand likely won't understand it at all. It's one of those faith things, where you trust that the Word of God is powerful, and is not returning void.

The same man in the story had two sons who memorized the entire Bible. Yes, the whole thing. Unbelievable. When they were asked **how** they did it, they said, *"Well, we really didn't* *spend a lot of time purposely memorizing it. We just heard it so much that it came natural!"*

Memorizing Scripture, then, is a powerful by-product of simply reading it regularly. A few years ago I took several longer passages of Scripture, put them to music and recorded *By Heart Scripture Songs CD (www.generationcedar.com/main/ our-products/scripture-cd)*. It made memorizing them a cinch!

In addition to reading and memorizing Scripture, we feel it is important to be able to point to Scripture for any offense our children commit. If they are being rude at the dinner table, it is not enough that they are corrected because they are causing me frustration. They should be reminded that rudeness is a breaking of the greatest command — to love your neighbor as yourself — and ultimately that is why we practice manners. Any other offense can be directed to a Scriptural principle and should be foundational to their discipline.

Teach Them to be Self-Learners

It amazes me how many people believe that a proper education can only be achieved with an "expert" feeding the student information. If anything, I would consider this a grave disadvantage. The whole world is at our disposal for observation, study and exploration. To be taught that my knowledge is limited only to what another can teach me is, at best, depressing! But it's also wrong. One of our main objectives is to show our children **how** to learn — where to find answers, and how to discover solutions. If a student can be led to the tools he needs to answer his own questions, he will be always learning; **and this should be the goal of every educator.**

Don't worry about having your children memorize facts. I've already mentioned several times how we often overlook the simplest of things. I read a quote by Albert Einstein once that said, *"Why should I work to fill my brain with facts and figures when I can simply look them up when I need them?"* I try to look at things and ask "why" or "is this the best way", before I just assume everyone else is doing it right.

Practically speaking, it is important that a child be taught how to use a dictionary, a map, a thesaurus, a concordance, a library, the Internet, an encyclopedia, graphs, charts and tables. This "teaching" can occur quite naturally as he sees you using those things to find answers. If we are reading about a particular person, or maybe an animal, and we come across a country or region, I usually stop there and point it out on our map or globe. Just getting them familiar with geography in that way is an incredible learning tool. Remember, his curiosity is already guiding him. Make sure he knows how to satisfy it.

One of the most important aspects of finding answers is asking questions. Cultivate his interests, and encourage him to ask. And let him hear you asking others about things you wish to know. Never fail to be curious!

Cultivating the Thoughts

We want children who know how to think. Of course we want them to think from a biblical worldview, and to be able to discern, analyze and critique the information they encounter. One of the best ways to do this is to challenge them with particular scenarios and questions. When they express an opinion, press them to explain it further. And then play the "devil's advocate." Of course their age determines how far you can go with this exercise, but as they get older, help them develop their line of reasoning. Keep pushing them to defend their positions.

As they learn to better express themselves in written language, requiring essays in defense of their positions is a great idea. Dad can read them at the table and the family can further discuss lines of reasoning.

An overlooked tool for cultivating the thoughts is simply play and imagination. Building with Legos, assembling puzzles, any "brain" activity during play is a wonderful way to stimulate the mind. We look for these types of things when we purchase toys.

If you have access to a debate team, often parents find it helpful for their older children to participate in those. Any exercise that engages the mind and challenges the thoughts is a worthy one.

Effective Communication

We believe it extremely important that our children be able to express, verbally and in written form, their beliefs, ideas and values. We desire them to be articulate. Real power lies in the ability to effectively communicate to the world your thoughts. It may seem extreme, but nothing helps develop communication like getting rid of, or at least turning off the television. Other than movies, we simply don't watch TV. It both saves us from a lot of garbage **and** facilitates our need to communicate with each other. **It's probably the single best strategy for building family relationships.**

We use a number of practical methods to sharpen our children's communication skills. Of course, just the dialog I mentioned earlier goes a long way, but here are a few other tangible ways to perfect these skills:

1. Copy Work

We practice a simple exercise called **copy work**. It is simply the copying of some writing we deem to be worthy of imitating. We use the Bible, poetry, famous quotes, favorite books, etc. The youngest children copy a few words or line. The older children may

> *"To be able to be caught up into the world of thought—that is to be educated."*
>
> *Edith Hamilton*

copy a paragraph. The goal is to copy it just as it is written, being careful with punctuation, spelling and form.

Copying sharpens all the skills useful for language and at the same time, makes the student familiar with good writing. It is a practice our forefathers often used, and has been regarded a very important practice for improving writing skills.

Don't overlook the simplicity of listening and observing other great communicators. Whether it is a live lecture, sermon or play, or a DVD, copying others who are great at something is a master's way of learning.

2. Writing Thank You Notes

As soon as the children begin writing, I look for opportunities for them to write and send thank-you cards or letters to friends and family. This is every child's first writing experience in our family. (Most importantly, this also helps develop an attitude of gratefulness.)

3. Essays and Stories

As they get older, like I mentioned previously, writing essays to defend their convictions can be a great tool for strengthening their writing skills. Some of your children may show interest in writing fiction.

I have a daughter who loves to read and also write her own stories. I encourage her to be creative, show her how a thesaurus can help improve her work, and use her writing to observe areas she needs to work on (capitalization, spelling, etc.) For further writing incentive, get familiar with the Op-Ed pieces in your local newspaper and encourage your children to write one and send it in.

Be open to what your child loves, and allow him to write about those topics. Forcing a child to read and write about subjects that are of no interest to him will likely not inspire him. Find what he loves, and work around that.

4. Journal

Keeping a journal is a wonderful way to develop writing skills as well as encouraging your children to think and observe the world around them. Many a professional writer started by keeping a journal. It helps both the process of writing, and the developing of his thoughts.

5. Blog

There are differing opinions and I would caution you with this suggestion, but a blog is a fun way to stimulate the thinking skills and hone the writing skills of a student. They are free and easy to use. Be sure to teach how to type first, though! (It's a great motivator for typing.) Years ago my oldest started a Science/Creation type blog where she could also use her love of photography, posting pictures of things from nature that stimulated her, and then researching and writing about them. I think it really stretched her and grew her love of writing and learning.

6. A Love of Reading

Much of the work of educating our children is reduced if they can read well and enjoy it. There is little out of reach of the mind of one who reads. We try to cultivate not only a love of reading, but a love of good books. Charlotte Mason has coined the term "living books", referring to those books written by authors with a passion for their subject, and the ability to communicate it through good writing.

> *"With life-learning, there is no start or finish, no taking off, no being behind... just a constant readiness to learn something else."*
>
> *Kelly Crawford*

Reading is fundamental to a rich education, because it is primarily the vehicle through which all information is passed. We try to include even our littlest children when we read, no matter the difficulty of the reading material. We especially try to read the Bible each day, in the hearing of all our children. I would note, however, that some children will not naturally enjoy reading as much as others. This should be OK. We should also remember that **doing** is an important form of learning and some children will prefer doing over **reading** about doing.

A constant collection of books is a worthwhile endeavor, and can be done quite inexpensively if you know where to look. A great resource for knowing which books to collect is "Books Children Love." I always browse the thrift stores, especially for older edition books, which in my opinion, are better written. Sites such as Amazon and Ebay are also great places to find particular books. Listen to other suggestions and keep a running list of books you would like to add to your family library.

For the uninterested reader:

If you have a child who isn't as interested in reading, keep encouraging him. Be sure to let him see you read, and respond to what you're reading. In addition, try the following tips:

- Taking your kids to the library can be a great way to spark their reading interest. Let them pick out, with your oversight, several of their own books. I consider a trip to the library and a few hours diving into the books a very successful school day!

- Create a "reading nook." A blanket thrown over a table, a corner with a bean-bag and a basket of books — sometimes the environment can be an enticement.

- Remind him time and again, in a non-implying way, that books take us places; reading is our key to the world around us, and so on. Verbalize the importance of reading.

- As already mentioned, don't push him too far. Some children learn better by experience and hands-on learning. This needs to be OK with us.

One woman I know had a nine year old who showed very little reading interest, and actually could hardly read at all. The mother discovered her daughter's deepest interests, and then found an exciting book about that subject. She began to read it out loud to her daughter, but she would stop right in the middle of the most tantalizing part. The daughter became so exasperated with the interruptions, that she finally picked the book up and decided to learn how to finish it! She's loved reading since then.

Teaching them to be productive

Almost always overlooked as part of an education is the teaching of being productive and industrious. Simply put, how to utilize our resources, creating with our hands and heart, something that will bless another. This productivity can be as simple as cooking a meal, or as complicated as remodeling a house. The ultimate reason for productivity is to bring God honor and glory. On a practical level it should involve strengthening the family economy. Stretching resources, making homemade gifts, ministering to others with meals, work, or gifts, creating art — **we consider teaching our children to be creative and productive one of the most important things in life!**

I have a great friend who has established a full-blown ministry and business encouraging families in this area. In addition to creating and selling instructional DVDs on the homemaking arts, she teaches local classes as well. We are learning basic quilting, sewing, cake decorating, the ministry of hospitality, bread-making, gift-making, how to grow and use herbs, and many other useful skills. They have also added classes for young men as well. *TeachingGoodThings*.com is, in my opinion, a really good thing!

Grasp of Numbers

To be "numerate" is simply to understand how numbers work and be able to use them when needed. Life math is important as it defines the type of math most people use on a daily basis. Encouraging our children to work through basic challenges throughout the day goes a long way helping them to become numerate.

In the very early years, don't miss the simplest ways to teach your children math. Count out loud. Divide out loud. Cut an orange or apple or pizza in slices and explain fractions, even if they don't quite understand yet. You are laying the groundwork for building. Talk about math as it applies to daily problems.

Cooking is a great opportunity to learn fractions and multiplying. Any time you need something measured, let your children help and explain things as you go. Shopping in an excellent way to deal with numbers. Everyone needs to be able to figure out cost per unit, so he can make the best purchasing decision. Look for mathematical opportunities — they're everywhere!

Besides "life math", this is one area we sometimes implement a formal curriculum. Our family loves *School of Tomorrow*

> ## Idea Corner
> Lunch time is a great time for working on memorization. We try to keep an ongoing passage of Scripture or poem that I read aloud to the children during lunch. This way, we remember to be consistent.

curriculum, by Accelerated Christian Education. It is thorough, self-teaching, easy-to-use and I highly recommend it. I've also used Khan Academy, short, instructional You Tube videos.

However, once they've mastered a concept, I don't require them to spend lots of time doing problems. I just let them skip on.

Our priority for math, especially as our children get older, is giving them a solid foundation in life-economics. That is, they need to understand how money works, how interest works, and how spending habits influence our lives. We teach them about credit, the danger of debt and how to save effectively.

Because regardless of how well they learn higher math, this is where meaningful math intersects with real life in a way that will profoundly influence their peace and well-being.

You can spend time and money preparing your children to hold a high-paying job (and hope that comes to fruition), or you can teach him to be a wise steward of whatever he has. The wise steward will come out better every time, regardless of the type of job he ends up doing.

My math challenge

I recently challenged myself to answer why I was making my children do pages and pages of long division. Then I concluded, why long division at all? I have never worked a long division problem on paper. There are devices that make that process much faster and simpler. This is smart. Our children need to know **when to divide**, and the concept of **how it works**, but to spend time doing an archaic algorithm seems wasteful to me when there is so much to learn. We focus our older children on life math — budgeting, learning how interest works, how to save, how to make wise purchases—the things of math that will largely determine their financial peace or misery.

If and when they need to learn higher math, they will.

Culture

Culture encompasses the arts — music, drama, poetry, painting, sculpture — those things which nurture the part of us that deeply longs for beauty and order because we are made in the image of our Creator. **Don't leave it out!** It also presents wonderful opportunities to serve and bless others.

On the simplest level, make your home a place of beauty, and collect books, music, and décor with a richness of art. I try to play classical music throughout our day — music that is soothing and not distracting. I have also purchased several large books with drawings and paintings that I like to leave out for the children to look at (be careful with this!)

Sometimes we will pick an artist — a musician, painter or sculptor — and study him for a week or so. Videos are helpful to enrich a study like this. In fact, the Internet now offers almost any resource you need for free. Utilize that tool!

"A work of art is above all an adventure of the mind."

Eugene Ionesco

Keep your eyes open for concerts and performances in your area. Often a company will host a performance for students and the cost is minimal or even free. Expose them to a variety of instruments and music, and if you are able, buy instruments for them and let them experiment. As soon as you see an interest or gift, lessons are an investment worth making (the same goes for art lessons). If lessons aren't feasible due to cost or location, consider purchasing a how-to video. Lessons are not always necessary; our daughter is self-teaching the violin right now and doing quite well.

We are fortunate enough to have a circle of friends with many talented, musical children. Our families enjoy getting together and playing music together. Ultimately, the arts should be pursued from a desire to glorify the Lord through them. If your child shows an interests in drawing or painting, consider how his gift could be used to minister to a lonely relative, neighbor or friend. Perhaps your musical children could perform an informal concert for surrounding widows. Or your family could practice an a capella choir for that purpose. Always be asking yourself how yours and your child's gifts can be used for the Kingdom!

Don't forget to let your children create art. Drawing, painting, coloring, making crafts with Popsicle sticks, weaving a pot holder on a plastic loom, crocheting, singing—it doesn't really matter the venue, just let them **CREATE!**

As the members of this society lose the practice and skill of production and art, those of us cultivating it will give our children such advantage and opportunities. **In fact, children raised in a home where the importance of production and economy are taught hardly need depend on a college degree for their entrance into the workforce... they will become the workforce!**

Idea Corner

Some children enjoy documenting and doing hands-on projects. Let your children design notebooks to go along with particular interests. If they find planets fascinating, encourage them to collect pictures, quotes, facts, etc. and paste them into a notebook or 3-ring binder. This type of documentation not only strengthens what they are learning, but also serves as a record for their studies. You could also have them do a final presentation from their notebooks to relatives or friends to encourage their communication skills.

Chapter 4:
Practical Learning Ideas

Much of what we do to facilitate the love of learning in our children is simply make information available to them in several different forms. As I mentioned earlier: so much of the relaxed concept of learning just seems too simple to work. But it's not! Forget what you've been told about how complicated and structured and expensive a good education is. Educating children is actually very simple. They want to learn--provide them the necessary materials to do so.

Here are some practical ways to facilitate natural learning:

Leave interesting magazines lying around.

I love to look on Ebay for slightly older collections of educational magazines. Favorites are *Creation Magazine* and *Nature's Friend*, specifically for kids. I randomly choose one ever so often, and just leave it lying around for them to find and dive into. Magazine subscriptions make great Christmas gifts. The kids love waiting in the mail for their new magazine to arrive. Then listen to what interests them...if it's raccoons, find more information to give them.

Family reading

We try to keep a good book going as a read-aloud by Dad at night, either around the supper table or before bed. (Not having television reception helps this a lot!) We have learned so much through these readings. Heroes of the Faith books are some of our favorites. I have included a list of suggested reading at the end of this book.

Buy a telescope and microscope.

Remember, curious minds want to know about life around them — so equip them to learn!

Field guides

Field guides to plants, insects, animals, etc. are **such** a helpful resource. When the children want to know "What kind of tree is that?", simply open up the guide and find out. We just bought an edible plant book and a book about surviving in the wilderness. The kids are loving it!

Educational videos

Why not? These videos do wonders to pique the interests of my children. We recently subscribed to Netflix. The advantages are incredible. First of all, we no longer have to stand, browsing at all the vulgarity at the movie store. Secondly, there are so many more movie selections available. I can search for exactly what I want — a documentary on Nova Scotia, a movie about Mother Teresa, a movie about how glass is made — something I could never find at Blockbuster. And most importantly, no late fees! It costs about $10 a month, for as many movies as we wish to see. I almost always supplement a subject we are reading about with a movie or documentary related to it.

Field Trips

Perhaps one of the homeschooler's greatest advantage—look for interesting places to visit and tour. It doesn't have to be a formal field trip... any place can become a fun learning experience for the attentive parent. (Drive to the airport one

Think Outside the Classroom:

day and just pique a curiosity in airplanes, followed up by some books and a movie from the library.) If your children show a particular interest in a place you visit, don't forget the most important words: "Let's look it up!"

Art Supplies

Keep art supplies readily accessible to children, younger and older. Encourage them to draw pictures more than they color pictures already drawn. Encourage them to look at pictures other artists have drawn and copy them. Investigate other forms of art that might spark interest. I keep telling my husband I would like to invest in a potter's wheel...who knows?

The Internet

As careful as we have to be, the Internet is basically the world at your fingertips. Teach them how to find information in a safe way. When they ask a question you don't know the answer to, you are sure to find it on the Internet. I'm convinced the Internet alone could provide a solid, rich education.

Idea Corner

Keep boxes/bags/baskets of "imagination" toys on hand, easily accessible to children. Puzzles, blocks, "old-fashioned" toys (stacking toys, etc.) all make great learning tools for developing young minds!

Chapter 5:
Answers to Your Questions

"What if there are gaps in my child's education?"

First of all, there are gaps in any education. But if you're concerned that your child won't know the same things their schooled counterparts know, let me offer words of encouragement and suggestions. Keep in mind that a large part of a school day is spent on other activities besides learning. A homeschooler gets in a couple of hours what it may take all day for a classroom teacher to impart to her students.

Secondly, remember that a large part of what you were actually "taught" in school, you didn't remember beyond the test. It's more likely much of what your children are learning is going to "stick" since their curiosities are being fed. That's one of the main points of "relaxed" learning... we hope to ignite what's already there, which is what makes information sink in and stay. And that fact should relax you.

Thirdly, whatever "gaps" show up in a repertoire of knowledge can easily be filled at the needed time, especially if a child is taught how to learn. The knowledge that goes in is not nearly as important as the ability to be able to find it when needed (remember Einstein said that, not me!)

> *"I'm glad I was never sent to school; it would have rubbed off some of the originality."*
>
> *Beatrix Potter*

Another practical way to "keep up" with what their peers are learning if this is really important to you, is to apply the relaxed learning style using a text book corresponding to your child's age as a kind of guide as you explore subjects. You would simply look through the text books to see what other children your child's age are learning, and then direct your studies to those particular subjects. It's a little more confining, but will work great. Also, if you use this method, just don't be afraid to "venture from the course", missing good opportunities for spontaneous learning.

"What About Keeping Records?"

Many homeschool coverings require detailed records or reports from their families. And even if they don't, some just feel better having them. Make the record-keeping simple. Using a notebook, journal or three-ring binder, log the activities of the day, including any books read, activities, movies, trips, etc. Don't hesitate to write things that you think are "too small." Looking up things on the Internet, or in a dictionary is legitimate "research study skills"; tracing a map to follow the missionary's journey from the book you're reading is geography; taking a walk and coming back with a leaf to look up is science. Make it count! Regardless of the type of form your homeschool covering provides, you should be able to easily transfer your written records to it.

"Is There a Schedule?"

Some families, some moms, and some children need more structure than others. A schedule provides necessary structure, based on your family's needs. Structured and relaxed can go together, as long as you keep the big picture in mind. What is the structure for? Let the schedule be your guide, not your master. As the old wise saying goes, "Don't miss the forest for the trees."

We have a regular "sit down" time where the children do their math work, copy work, and reading or English. We also have regular intervals of read-alouds, or an older child reading to a younger one. It's OK to have a framework. Just be open to spontaneous learning moments when you see a spark! And don't forget to be constantly questioning, "Why are we doing this?" Challenge the status quo. If it's not a real education, toss it.

Also, because we consider learning to be constantly happening, all day, every day, all year, I don't get bent out of shape for missing this formal sit-down time. It's the difference in thinking of "school" vs. "education." If we are always learning, we are not missing anything and we're not behind.

"How Will a Child Learn Discipline With This Model?"

Many argue that this relaxed method will create haphazard or even lazy students. That in order to teach discipline, there must be a rigid schedule. It has been my experience there are lots of other opportunities to teach a child proper discipline and adherence to a schedule, especially in the area of chores and household responsibilities. And really, even though we learn in a relaxed way, our whole day is still confined within a schedule. There is order, even when we are exploring a subject. It doesn't make sense to me that just because the school schedule doesn't follow a bell, our children won't learn discipline. Life provides the natural framework for all the discipline one needs. Years ago, parents didn't fret about this aspect. Learning was far more natural, and so was learning to be disciplined.

"What about Standardized Testing and College?"

I know many families practicing the relaxed method of schooling (and even "unschooling") whose children have scored exceptionally high on standardized tests. Again, you may want to follow an outline out of a textbook to make sure you cover things expected to be on a test. You may also find practice tests on-line to assess testability. Colleges actively seek homeschooled students. Keep a journal or record of your studies, and you will likely have no trouble at all with entrance.

Additionally, more and more families are rethinking the over-emphasis placed on having a college degree. Many companies are seeing the benefit of other credentials besides a paper in hand. A **portfolio** can be a weighty addition to the homeschooler's arsenal. Keeping track of any on-the-job training, on-line courses, extra classes, etc. can be as convincing as a diploma... most likely more!

Chapter 6:
Relaxed Homeschooling Articles (From Kelly's blog)

Reading to Your Children May Be More Important Than You Think

"If we would only consider the subtle strengthening of ties which comes from two people reading the same book together, breathing at once its breath and each giving the other unconsciously his interpretation of it, it would be seen how, in this simple habit of reading aloud, lies a power too fine to analyze, yet stronger than iron in welding souls together. To our thinking, there is no academy on earth equal to that found in so many homes, of a mother reading to her child."

Elisha Schudder,
The Riverside Magazine for Young People

Reading is good, everyone knows that. It enriches your thought life, aids your reasoning, enhances your communication, and in general, educates the mind.

But what if that is only the beginning?

A Family Program for Reading Aloud provokes me to think that maybe reading aloud to my children is more beneficial to our relationship than even their education.

Think Outside the Classroom:

Here's another excerpt from the book:

"American Christian parents began to lose control over their children when they relinquished home reading aloud. As they turned over the education of their children to outside agencies, even to the Sunday School and to the Christian School, they lost a critical part of their intimate relationship with their children. Many wonderful teachers have gained by what parents let go—yet parents alone have opportunities which are never afforded to those outside the realm of home."

Consider that Jesus said, *"A good man out of the good treasure of his heart brings forth what is good... out of the abundance of the heart his mouth speaks."* **(Luke 6:45)**

Home was once the place where hearts could be filled with "good treasure", and reading played a significant part in that. Good literature was an integral part of the Christian home and the formation of character depended much on parents reading and instilling the love of reading in their children.

If we relinquish our commitment to intentionally form the mind and hearts of our children toward what is good and noble, we give it to someone else — other influences and voices fighting for their allegiance.

It seems almost old fashioned to talk about rekindling the practice of reading aloud as a family, because I fear our digital age is an unintentional enemy of that fundamental habit of gathering together, all our faculties focused on the same story, our attention directed and unified toward a common theme.

Read to your children if you do nothing else. Reading to them will grow your hearts together, enlarge their imaginations, plant something wonderful in their memories and gradually refine their characters as they turn into men and women.

The Ultimate Cheat Sheet
for a Complete (Christian) Education

James Altucher wrote a counter, jaw-dropping piece entitled, *"The Ultimate Cheat Sheet on Having a Complete Education"*, in which he said such antithetical things like:

> "Let's take it subject by subject: SCIENCE.
>
> You actually need to know NOTHING.
>
> Biology textbooks are hopelessly outdated. As are physics textbooks. There are better resources online where you can learn faster without the pressure of tests and homework. But unless you are doing CPR soon, you don't need to know anything.
>
> Nobody remembers the muscle names five minutes after the test is over. Unless you are a chiropractor or a surgeon, when was the last time you made use of basic biology?"

I agreed with much of what he wrote, and disagreed with some of it, probably because of our different worldviews.

So I decided to write my own **"Ultimate Cheat Sheet"**, borrowing from Altucher's common sense but reflecting my Christian beliefs, foundational to how we approach education.

Subject by subject:

1. Math

I like what Altucher said:

> *"I've been a computer programmer, an entrepreneur, an investor, day trader, etc. All areas that needed "math." The highest level of math I needed to know in the past twenty-five years… Percentages."*

Only I would add:

Finance, as in how to flesh it out in real life, is of supreme importance. Regardless of the level of math one completed, the majority of Americans are in terrible financial trouble, swaggering under debt, and their lives, regardless of income, are ruled by dismal financial failures from poor life decisions.

Most math is best learned as life necessitates it. A carpenter becomes fluent in geometry, not because he was studious in class, but because geometry is real to him and is necessary to his job.

Be numerate. The rest will come as needed.

2. History

Altucher:

> *"First thing: Forget everything they teach you in school. None of it is correct, OR none of it you will remember. Probably all of it is lies."*

I think he's right. Real, "living" history books and documentaries, that's the way to go. And discussions about them. And visits to museums when the chance avails itself. And awesome resources like my friend's new project, "Under Drake's Flag", where real history comes to life.

3. Science

Health and nutrition will benefit you as much as anything. Beyond that, though, a cursory study of whatever interests you serves to reveal the glory of God and His infinite power. You can't learn it all, that's for sure. So, learn what interests you. Get out in the physical world. Look around and ask questions. Then find the answers. Unless you want to become a surgeon. Then learn more.

4. English

The grand goal is communication. Learning to communicate well will cover a multitude of deficiencies. How to achieve this? Copy others who do it well. It's the best way to learn almost anything. Vocabulary, proper grammar usage and punctuation, how to use words–it's all done best by listening to, and copying those who do it better. Along these lines I would suggest that children don't learn much from other children, including how to use words.

5. Typing

Everyone should learn to type.

But the most important part of a complete education?

Well, it's not a subject at all, but far more useful than anything a curriculum can offer is the study of wisdom.

> *"Blessed are those who find wisdom, those who gain understanding, for she is more profitable than silver and yields better returns than gold."*
>
> *Proverbs 3:13-14*

Which is preceded by the fear of the Lord.

> *"The fear of the Lord is the beginning of wisdom and knowledge of the Holy One is understanding."*
>
> **Proverbs 9:10**

Wisdom will ensure better financial success than you think a college degree will.

Here's an ideal curriculum:

- Copy from the Bible, length of passage according to age. Copy poetry. Copy old books.

- Hang out with adults. A lot. Especially wise ones.

- Read. Then tell someone about what you read.

- Write. Write letters, write on a blog, write to the newspaper, write in a journal. Especially write a thank you letter once a week. Have someone edit for grammar and punctuation. Use a thesaurus. Learn a new word and tell your family about it at dinner.

- Write more. Take a few sentences from your local newspaper and rewrite them using half the words. Learn to say things concisely, without using extra words.

- Watch videos about how things are made. Or about cooking. Or about things you like. Read books about the same things.

- Find someone doing what you love and ask to watch or help them.

- Learn how to do something new.

- Ask questions. Do puzzles. Listen to sermons. Play Scrabble, Moneywise, Monopoly and other learning games.

- When you read about a country, go to the map and find it.

- Start a business. Start a blog. Find ways to make money.

How Will Your Kids be Prepared for the Real World (Unless They Go to School There?)

It's the number one opposition homeschoolers face from doubting questioners, and unfortunately, one of the biggest obstacles preventing parents from deciding to homeschool: parents want their children to be prepared for the real world so they think they must send them to school.

Stop: who got us to think upside down? Essentially, what this means is, we feel like the best way to prepare our children for the real world is to take them out of the real world, put them in an unrealistic world all day for twelve years, try to simulate the real world, and then tell everyone this is the only way to prepare them for the real world. It's hilarious just writing that out!

> *"Bill Gates recently gave a speech at a High School about 11 things they did not and will not learn in school. He talks about how feel-good, politically correct teachings created a generation of kids with no concept of reality and how this concept set them up for failure in the real world."*
>
> **Resource for Kids**

All I want to do here is to help people who want to homeschool but are gripped with this irrational fear to "let it go!" This is not an attempt to put down anyone, but to offer a discerning look at an often misunderstood topic. If you're happy with the simulated circumstance (and many are), this isn't about convincing you to homeschool.

However, we should all want to talk and think like rational humans so for the sake of everyone who must make this important life decision about educating his child, we at least need to make it based on the facts and truth of reality. It's a bit like my choice to bottle feed my first baby. I knew I would have to go to work and I was still in school and so I decided to bottle feed because I didn't see a way to breast feed. I did not, however, pretend bottle feeding was better or even the same as nursing in order to justify my decision. I knew it was second best, but it was the decision I felt I had to make. Regardless of our decisions, we need to at least be honest about them.

How schools must recreate the real world

In the first several years of school, especially, a classroom must try to recreate real life which is hardly possible, making the classroom second best for real learning. That's not an insult, it's simply a truth, like saying real hair is preferable to a wig. Exploration, creativity, freedom, hands-on learning, it is all greatly limited if not extinguished, in the classroom.

> *"Tell me and I'll forget; show me and I may remember; involve me and I'll understand."*

I was thinking about this as my 5 year old asked me what time it is. I've never given my children clock worksheets–we have a clock on the wall. And when they begin to be aware of time and the clock, I show them, until they understand, how time works. That's it. They all learn to tell time. (Same way they learned the English language.)

We don't even have phonics books. We use phonics as we sit down with books together, sounding out letters, blends and memorizing sight words, and eventually, they begin reading.

We don't read books about "opposites" or colors, or numbers; all those things exist in our daily conversations and children are remarkable learners. It comes naturally in real life. We learn about vegetation outside, we classify real birds and real trees when we go for walks. We talk about current events at the dinner table, asking probing questions that require thought and analytic skills.

We discuss lifestyles and how to handle different situations after we leave events, family gatherings, or vacations.

Life teaches

Hygiene from a health book? No. Weather? It's there.

Is it reading about the solar system (a perfectly wonderful thing to do) or would the words come alive if they were just given a telescope and notepad to chart their observations?

Another unrealistic thing (necessary only for keeping order and tracking of large groups) is the idea of "school in" or "school out", deadlines, and grade levels. I could write a book, but suffice it to say, it's optimal to embrace learning (i.e. "school") as something always happening, without the confines of time and space. We will never learn all there is to learn; why not develop a mindset of always-learning what is in front of us and what we need to know to enhance our gifts?

As they get older, what then? Is real life being confined to rooms lined with desks and people the same age with little time for conversation and interpersonal exchange? Or is it being allowed to mingle, in the real world, observing and attempting adultish things? Exploring all their interests? Following their passions? Figuring things out on their own?

Do we "sit down and do school", ever? Yes, but not because it's necessary. We mostly read a lot, I give writing assignments and go over those for proper grammar and usage, the older ones have a formal math curriculum (I'm tweaking this a lot) and they do copy work. Most everything though, can be and is being learned in the context of real life. There are far more pressing things than whether our children can recall the area of a trapezoid (Google it if you need it!)

Keep in mind, the evidence consistently shows that qualities employers desire (if the goal is to work for someone else) hardly ever include test scores or the ability to memorize facts, etc. It's almost always about character, communication skills and the ability to solve problems–all most easily learned in the real world, where children are free to satisfy their curiosities and find solutions, an amazing trait the Creator gave us all when we were born. In fact, even most highly specialized jobs provide on-the-job training, requiring the capacity for learning, not a specific set of facts already learned (which most students forget anyway).

Yes, I know there are those needed jobs where students must still jump through the hoops of the system (achieving certain test scores, etc., homeschooled or otherwise). Thankfully though, even this is being widely reconsidered as the job industry is discovering how a college degree or other "certification" may not always be a comprehensive representation of a person's expertise. More and more are seeing the benefits of apprenticeship/hands-on training.

If you worry about your children learning to cope in the real world, I don't blame you; consider homeschooling them.

Importance of the Family Table
(With a Look at Educational Benefits)

We already know research backs up the notion that families eating around the table together has a profound impact on the quality of home and the unity of its members.

An article in the Home Renaissance Foundation said,

> *"...family dinners generate 'human capital'. Kids who sit down regularly with parents and siblings do better at exams than those who don't. Rates of substance abuse, obesity and eating disorders are also lower....It is at the dining table that we impart some of the most important lessons of life: how to tell a story, share our recollections of the day and listen politely. It is where kids should learn something about manners. Not formal etiquette, but how to behave in company. It is easy to dismiss these things as irrelevant."*

Bridges & Tangents

And this from "Meals and Food":

> *"Eating together, each day, without the TV or computer on, can bring so many blessings to family life. It gives your children time with you, and time with each other. It allows you to listen, to talk, and to share things. It gives rhythm and regularity to each day, and to the week – which is so important for the children. It puts the brakes on the constant rushing of modern life. Eating together gives space for personalities to grow, for language to develop, for ideas to emerge. It gives a simple way of praying together, if you say grace before meals, and pray in thanksgiving after them. And you make sure that the children are eating well!"*

Think Outside the Classroom:

But even beyond these important reasons families should make breaking bread together a priority, the table affords incredible learning opportunities with a little deliberate attention.

Here are a few ideas to ignite conversation and discussion, key components in a real education:

- Read an article from the newspaper and ask each one (who is old enough) if he agrees, why or why not, or some other questions pertinent to the article.

- Read a passage of Scripture and then a commentary about it (we love Matthew Henry's). You could also have your children "narrate" or tell back what you read.

- Keep an educational/interesting facts "table book" handy and read an excerpt from it.

- Incorporate art at the table. Show a different work of art each night and ask the children to offer some interpretation about it, or read about the artist and the history of the work.

- Prepare pieces of paper ahead of time with "Did you know" facts on them. Fold them, put them in a bowl in the middle of the table, and each night a different child can take turns drawing one and sharing it.

I would love to know if your family has any ideas to make the most of table talk!

Rethinking Education:
The Overrated College Degree
Drives the System... & Apprenticeship

"I don't think we'll get rid of schools any time soon, certainly not in my lifetime, but if we're going to change what's rapidly becoming a disaster of ignorance, we need to realize that the institution "schools" very well, but it does not "educate"; that's inherent in the design of the thing. It's not the fault of bad teachers or too little money spent. It's just impossible for education and schooling to be the same thing."

John Taylor Gatto

Changing the way we think about education is difficult because we have been conditioned to **fear.**

The whole chain of education is linked with fear. We want our kids to have a "good education" but we've let big business define what that means. Because we don't really mean a "good education" or we would all oppose the current system. What we really mean is "a good-paying job" and the system was created, from the top down, to function the way it does to lock us in by fear.

"...students hear again and again that a degree from a special college is such a powerful advantage in later life that the quarter-million dollar cost is fully justified...if you are one of the lucky ones who can afford it.

Skip over the morality of this contention. As a statement of fact, it's a masterpiece of fabrication – scientifically speaking on par with the medieval theory of four humors. If it appears true, it's a tribute

Think Outside the Classroom:

to ceaseless propaganda because the employment game has been heavily rigged to make it seem so and because critics of the enchantment are marginalized as screwballs... A degree from a highly ranked school hardly matters at all in the real world; it only matters to people who believe the lie..."

John Taylor Gatto,
Don't Worry About College,
A Letter to My Granddaughter
(I highly recommend this brilliant piece.)

To get a "good job", a student needs a college degree (so we think). To get a college degree he needs good ACT scores. To get those, he needs good test scores in school. That's really what the majority of parents care about.

And so the system is increasingly loyal to a test, betraying the individual student's passion and need for learning what matters.

(And I interject, again, that those of us who homeschool have the tremendous opportunity to escape this hamster wheel, and yet all too often I see frazzled moms desperately trying to recreate the broken model at home.)

Apprenticeship

The good news is, there are new (but actually not new) possibilities on the horizon and **finally**, employers are beginning to seek out employees with skills they don't necessarily learn in college.

Apprenticeships are making a big comeback and this is GREAT news if you are opposed to the assembly-line education like we've been discussing.

A UK publication reports:

"Apprenticeships have changed. From the days of a novice learning his trade at the side of a master craftsman, they have evolved to include high-tech specialised programmes in nuclear physics and high-end training with bespoke designer fashion labels.

They should no longer be considered the poor relation of university study or the last resort for those not cut out for formal education.

Big businesses look to them as key to developing the expertise and skills needed to grow their workforce..."

The Raconteur

Now we get back to the real basics of an education:

- an eager learner
- a good communicator
- problem-solver
- critical thinker
- analytical
- motivated self-learner

"Apprenticeships have gotten a new lease on life," said Anthony Carnevale, chief economist of the American Society for Training and Development in Alexandria, Va. "They're extending beyond white males with calluses on their hands to a variety of people and occupations. We need more highly skilled workers."

The Seattle Times

Please don't misunderstand me. There is a place for a traditional college degree. If one of my children **needs** a college degree, we would not be opposed to that route. The aim here is to overturn the general, damaging mindset that "everyone must get a college degree."

Besides the tremendous debt students often find themselves in, a large percentage of kids have no reason for attending college besides "my parents want me to" or "that's what everybody does."

I debated about doing a whole post devoted to "the problem with college" but I'll let you investigate more on that subject if you wish. This article in the Wall Street was quite practical with lots of good examples: College is a Scam.

Suffice it to say, until we destroy the myth that "college is the answer for everyone", we will continue to let fear drive our methods, largely robbing our children of a potentially better education.

An Example: My brother

There have been several excellent examples in the comment sections (on the first two parts of this series) of people whose skills won out over a missing college degree in the work force. Another such one is my brother, who is the perfect example in this discussion…

Had Chris not been squeezed into the mold, it's hard to say where his interests and gifts would have taken him. He is an artist, but "art isn't a very practical skill" so he wasn't encouraged much. He got through high school, rather hating academics but enduring them like everyone else, far more concerned with his peers and weekend activities than his homework.

But Chris did have a head start, thanks to some of the early experiences we had as children, including learning to communicate well. Our Dad, who is very wise and discerning, also passed that down to my brother and made quite a critical thinker out of him. And work ethic…if there's one thing my Dad believes is important…

Chris didn't go to college. He did apprentice under a Civil Engineer for a while and then decided he wanted to get his pilot license. He learned all he needed for that because it interested him and he was motivated.

Later, he applied for a highly-specialized job at an aviation navigation company in CO. He trained first as a data analyst, beating dozens of applicants more "qualified" with degrees, because the employer saw skills in him that were valued above a piece of paper. Later he was promoted to supervisor in Navigation Data Extract, involving global communications and the coordinating of teams world-wide.

Now he is a top Realtor in his area, again out-performing many of his more "qualified" colleagues. He is respected by his peers, both personal and professional. He's very entrepreneurially minded too, and often does web design work on the side. He does all this, by the way, with near-perfect humility. But I'm not biased.

We chatted about the discussion I wanted to have here on the blog. He said, "You know, it really does boil down to a few things…if you can think, if you know how to learn, and if you can communicate well and (he emphasized this one), know how to relate to people with integrity, there's not much you can't do that you want."

I think he's right.

Think Outside the Classroom:

An Open Letter of Apology to My Former High School Student

Dear Jacob,

I taught you in English class when you were eighteen years old and I owe you an apology. In fact, all your teachers do.

I bought the lie and I lied to you, and it had a profoundly negative impact on you.

I told you that since you weren't interested in dissecting Shakespeare, you wouldn't amount to much in life. Oh I didn't say it in those exact words, but close.

I remember taking you into the hallway–I know you remember it too (shame on me for shaming you) and telling you that "successful people pay attention and do well in class and study and make good grades."

Your eyes filled with tears because that news must have been a crushing blow. (I can't imagine being told that if I didn't paint as well as the others in my art class, I wasn't as good as them, and doomed to a life of failure.)

That's what we're all brainwashed to believe. That's what the "smart" people say, and no one really sees how stupid it is. That grades are what makes someone successful? How were we even convinced of such nonsense?

You were smart. You were smart in a hundred ways but we used our tiny little measuring stick in our tiny little boxes and the ones who refused to jump through our tiny little hoops were made to feel stupid.

Thousands of children still suffer every day the way I made you suffer.

You knew back then what I refused to see. That there is nothing normal or productive about forcing energetic, curious boys to sit in desks all day and force-feed them Chaucer. Some are even being drugged to sit there. Perfectly wonderful boys, sedated to act like something they aren't, to waste valuable time on a lecture they won't remember when they could be learning so much more–stuff that will really give them a good life. I can't believe we sit by and let it happen.

You didn't need Chaucer.

You needed freedom. You needed to work with your hands and do what you were good at. To improve those skills that were uniquely yours and uniquely wonderful and just as important as writing essays.

And you needed us to tell you that. To say that there are a thousand ways to be smart. Some people do love Chaucer and some people love taking a car apart and putting it back together. Both of those things are good and needful and should receive equal attention and affirmation.

We told you it was good and normal to be isolated from real life all day in small cells, requiring permission to even go to the bathroom. You were a man and you couldn't go to the bathroom unless I let you! We used bells to program you to stop and start on command, essentially saying that nothing is worth pouring your time and energy into until it's finished.

We told you we were the experts and we defined "success" and we got to stamp your card for life to tell the world you were either a "good student" or a "bad student."

Jacob, I am so ashamed to have claimed to be helping children, all the while hurting you and many others.

You survived despite our efforts to keep you confined within that box. That's what the human spirit does. But I'm sure you would have been so much better off without us.

Well I'm different now, Jacob. I fight, in my little corner of the world, for people like you. For people like my own children— for the majority of children who are having their creativity, their originality, their unique gifts and interests crushed by those they trust.

Please forgive me. And don't buy the lie. I was wrong. They are wrong.

There is an alternative to forced-schooling.
Think Outside the Classroom.

"Schools are for showing off, not for learning. When we enroll our children in school, we enroll them into a never ending series of contests—to see who is best, who can get the highest grades, the highest scores on standardized tests, win the most honors, make it into the most advanced placement classes, get into the best colleges. We see those grades and hoops jumped through as measures not only of our children, but also of ourselves as parents. We find ways, subtly or not so subtly, to brag about them to our friends and relatives. All this has nothing to do with learning, and, really, we all know it."

Dr. Peter Gray,
Schools Are Good For Showing Off,
Not for Learning

Resources

The Internet contains all the information for an endless education. However, we limit the amount of time our children spend viewing the screen, and we carefully monitor their access. But used properly, it can be an invaluable resource. If your budget is tight, there are enough resources here that you shouldn't have to spend a dime on anything else. Even coloring pages, copy work sheets, math practice pages and tests are available for free printing. These are some of our favorites:

Starfall *(www.starfall.com)*: great site for phonics and reading
All-in-One Homeschool *(www.allinonehomeschool.com)*
Khan Academy *(www.khanacademy.org)*
TLS Books *(www.tlsbooks.com)*: free printable sheets
YouTube / Netflix: a great place to look for videos to correspond with your studies
Answers.com: a sort of on-line encyclopedia and dictionary
Kid Zone *(www.kidzone.ws)*: information site
Ebooks Read *(www.ebooksread.com)*: download free ebooks

Great Books
I could list a bunch, but here are a few to get you started:

Ten Peas in a Pod
Lamplighter's Series
The Light & the Glory by Peter Marshall
A Different Kind of Teacher by John Taylor Gatto
The Kingdom Series by Chuck Black
The Pilgrim's Progress by John Bunyan
When Science Fails by John Hudson Tiner
For Those Who Dare by John Hudson Tiner
Shakespeare Tales by Charles and Mary Lamb
Trial & Triumph by Richard Hannula
Fifty Famous Stories Retold by James Baldwin
When You Rise Up by R.C. Sproul Jr.
Christian Heroes: Then & Now by Geoff and Janet Benge

About the Author

Kelly and her husband Aaron homeschool their ten children and have a passion for encouraging and strengthening families in the Lord. Kelly formerly taught high school English and Drama. Combining her writing passion, her love of God and family and an entrepreneurial vision, she created Generation Cedar *(www.generationcedar.com)*, the blog where those things all come together. A freelance writer for various magazines, websites, books and ebooks, she also occasionally speaks at homeschool and ladies' conferences.

More Ebooks from Kelly
(www.generationcedar.com/main/our-products/ebooks):
    When Motherhood Feels Too Hard
    Finding Financial Freedom
    Getting Your Children to Obey
    How to Make & Sell Your Own Skin Products
    Easy Health for Busy Moms
    Simple Cooking to Save You Money

Help with Scripture Memorization:
    Listen to our Scripture Songs CD
    (www.generationcedar.com/main/our-products/scripture-cd)

Visit our blog:
    Generation Cedar *(www.generationcedar.com)*

Made in the USA
Lexington, KY
20 July 2016